REVITALIZING INSPIRATIONAL THOUGHT CONDITIONERS

A helpful spiritual guide with strategies and tips to obtain unspeakable Joy through positive thinking!!!

by
Bestselling Author
Jan F. Whitaker

Unless otherwise indicated all scriptural quotations are taken from the King James Version of the Bible.

50 Revitalizing Inspirational Thought Conditioners
Copyright © 2012
Jan F. Whitaker

Printed in the United States of America

Library of Congress – Catalogued in Publication Data

ISBN 978-0-9839248-5-2

<u>Editorial Service</u>
Jabez Books Writers' Agency
(A Division of Clark's Consultant Group)
www.clarksconsultantgroup.com

FOREWORD

Who knows whether God has brought Jan Whitaker into the kingdom for such a time as this?

"All of life is a heart matter." The Word of God declares that we are to keep our heart with all diligence, because out of it proceeds the issues of life. The United Negro College Fund says, "A mind is a terrible thing to waste."

In the last and evil days; evil men and seducers shall wax worse and worse, deceiving and being deceived; and many will have itching ears and be led away, falling from their own steadfastness. In other words, their minds will be overloaded with foolishness and no substance to live by.

So, thank you, Jan, for calling our attention back to God's Word and showing us our need to hide it in our heart that we might not sin against Him. This powerful book is a refreshing second look at these fifty chosen scriptures that will strengthen the sword of the spirit in the hand of the believer and equip him to live everyday triumphantly in God's presence.

God's word teaches us that He will keep us in perfect peace if we keep our mind stayed on him, and trust in Him (Isa. 26:3 ABV). Now more than ever before, God's people need that solace that only His Word can give to us.

This book is a must read for every serious Christian, as it will certainly revitalize, inspire and condition our hearts for greater things in God's kingdom.

Much love, peace and strength to you, Jan Whitaker, and your family.

In God's love,

Bishop Fred A. Caldwell, Sr.
Pastor/Teacher
Greenwood Acres Full Gospel B.C.
Shreveport, LA

Endorsements

In this extraordinary book Sister Whitaker explains that life is not your enemy, but your thinking can be. She reminds us that our mind is a very powerful tool that can work for us or against us at any given moment. It's a must read!

Mary K. Caldwell, Greenwood Acres Full Gospel B.C.-First Lady

Everyone was born to make a deposit in their generation. If you die full, you did not deposit your gift. I thank God, our Father for Jan making her deposits in her generation. May this spiritual guide enrich your life and as God blesses you, may you be a blessing and make your deposits into the lives of others to the glory of God.

Advancing His Kingdom,
Your Sister, Kathryn Renee Williams

This spiritual guidebook will guide you through a divine transformation back to God.

I thank God for keeping you above ground to help His word to get out. You are a great mouth piece for God!!!! That's the compliment that describes you best.PRAISE GOD FOR A WOMAN NAME JAN!!!!! Love you!!!

Author, Beatrice L. Brown

Life is always considered to be full of challenges, but the way you handle the challenges will determine if the result is destructive or productive. Jan Whitaker's Spiritual Guide will definitely direct you to productive thinking, and you will be a better person from it.

Author, RaShad D. Bristo

Glory to the Most High!!! The writer lets us know that life is a journey, stay on the road. Life is really whatever you make of it, follow your dream and stick to it. If you're going to believe in something, believe in yourself, stay humble, encourage others and don't forget to always encourage yourself. Thank you, Jan, for speaking to us about going through situations that are particularly bad, but after getting through it, you'll discover that you have more strength than you ever had. Thanks, Jan. May God richly bless you.

Regards Lucius L. Farris, Brother

Jan has written another very powerful and encouraging book.

Juanita F. Harbor, Best Friend

Jan is such a great inspiration and co-labourer for the sake of the Gospel. Her enthusiasm and altruism is nothing short of a miracle to everyone she touches. You will not be disappointed, but refreshed all the more by Jan's books.

Best Regards,
Minister Draper Wright

Jan's new book is very inspirational and unique. This book is very uplifting and is a Magnificent read from a wonderful author!

Sherman Fuller-College student

Jan's book will help bring you to a place of solitude in your life where you will find peace even in the valley.

Joyce Burrell, Team Leader

Jan's book is a must read for anyone who want to know the real deal about living a Joyous Christian life.

Janet Jackson, Author

You are a blessing to the body of Christ and I am so glad God hooked us up as friends, and no my name is not Ruth, but where you go I will go. Your God will always be my God. This new book God gave you to write to help others is a blessing. You can have what you say.

Minister (Author) Gregory L. White

You were a blessing to me our first time meeting at the National Black Book Festival. You are a Victorious Woman of GOD!! I thank God for you!!

Author, Rowena Jackson

I would suggest to everyone to run, don't walk to pick up your copies of Jan's latest book, **50 Revitalizing Inspirational Thought Conditioners**. It is a must read. I just love having a Bestselling Author as a Sister.

Love you.
Shirley Farris Thomas, Sister

Jan has taken into great detail what is sometimes suppressed by Christians and that is the power of our thoughts. Our thoughts form our words and this can be seen in Jan's book, **"50 Revitalizing Inspirational Thought Conditioners."** This book will truly impart knowledge and change. If you would open up your heart and receive these blessings from God, your life will never be the same.

Gwendolyn Clark-RN

Jan's publication will touch your heart and warm your spirit!

Lisa Myers
Principal and Best Friend

God speaks; Ms. Jan listens, obeys, and writes. Reading Ms. Jan's instructions and obeying them explicitly cause regenerated lives. Continue listening, experiencing, obeying, and writing, Ms. Jan.

Dr. Carrie M. Williams

When wisdom speaks, treat the words of wisdom as you would do a good food that enters the mouth. Savor the words of wisdom in this book as they enter your spiritual ear. Never refuse wisdom, for she will guide you to the fruitful places of life.

Author, Marilyn Reed

This is an awesome book from a fantastic author! Inspiration and guidance are very much needed in this day and age. Thank God for using people like my mother, Jan F. Whitaker to do so.

Korey Duane Whitaker, Son

<u>INTRODUCTION</u>

Since joy depends upon the kinds of thoughts we think, it is absolutely impossible to be joyful if we think unhappy thoughts that are non-productive.

Even Solomon, with all his strength, God made him one of the wisest men that ever lived. But even after God gave Him clear instructions not to marry women from foreign nations, he chose to disregard God's commands.

Through Solomon's disobedience he married not one, but many heathen wives, who subsequently led him away from God (1 Kings 11:2). What about you? Is there something or someone that you are allowing to lead you away from God? If you answered truthfully to this question, then this book is definitely for you. God knows our strengths and weaknesses, and His commands are ALWAYS for our good.

This publication of "50 Revitalizing Inspirational Thought Conditioners" is designed to help strengthen and protect your weakest areas in your life because a chain is only as strong as its weakest link.

It is not enough to know God's Word or even to believe it; we must follow it and apply it to life's daily activities and decisions. We need to ALWAYS take God's commands seriously.

Many people today ignore God's commands, but negative consequences inevitably result. For in all of his wisdom, Solomon had some weak spots, just as we all do. He could not say "NO" to compromise or to lustful desires. Whether he married to strengthen political alliances or to gain personal pleasure, these foreign wives led him into idolatry. I said that to say this, we may have strong faith, but we also have weak spots--and it is there, that temptation usually strikes. In my experience of many years in working with people, I have found that the most

14

truthful, powerful, vital, and positive thoughts are those stated in the Bible from the Holy scriptures from the Word of God.

The Words of God are alive and active in all believers. The scriptures itself states what God's Word will do in our life. *If ye abide in Me and My words abide in you ye shall ask what ye will, and it shall be done unto you* (John 15:7). This simply means if we saturate our mind and heart with God's Holy Word, it will become so embedded that God's Word will sink from our conscious to our subconscious mind. Therefore, we will become so conditioned in our personality with spirituality, with spiritual POWER and sensitivity that God's will can operate in us.

Every wonderful and great value in this life, the ones that are beneficial, can be yours, just for the asking. The words of the Bible are "POWERFUL" refreshing thought conditioners. They are capable of revolutionizing our entire personality.

Over the years, I have recommended certain passages both personally and in counseling to others. The Word say, <u>If a brother or sister are overtaken in a fault, ye which are spiritual,</u> (notice the Word distinctively says spiritual and not religious) restore such a one in the spirit of meekness (see Galatians 6:1).

It would be wonderful if you will commit these scriptures to memory. Therefore, you will have them there as a sort of spiritual food pantry, each to be drawn out as needed for what ails us or to meet life situations head-on as they develop. I suggest you use these passages of scriptures, or "POWERFUL" refreshing thought conditioners" over and over again. It does not matter what you are doing. Whether it's at home, work, on an airplane, in a car, washing clothes, doing the dishes, or waiting at the doctor's office, meditate on the meaning of what you have read. As you do, they will be like a refreshing straight wave of truths. Gradually they will strengthen your mind until your life will become a living demonstration of God's power. When I applied these scriptures to my own life, I found they indeed possess tremendous effectiveness and has accomplished more impressive results.

I believe this is a good time to share a few of the results that came about in my life, so you will know that God's Word really work for those who want it to work. Anyway, since I asked God to change my way of thinking through His Word, He has manifested many blessings in my life.

God healed me from cancer, fibromyalgia, death of my father, mother, and son at age 25, gambling addiction, and depression, to name some, but He just keeps on blessing me. He ordained for me to write books to help others, and then turned around and made me a Bestselling Author, and gave me my own radio show, all for His Glory. You see, we have to keep all these things that God give us in prospective. It's not for us, it's for God's glory, and for others to let them know

17

that they, too, can have those things as well if they use these same God-given Kingdom principles.

Matthew 6:33 tells us, "But seek ye first the kingdom of God, and His righteousness; and all these things shall be added unto you." This guide contains 50 POWERFUL and VITAL passages. Someone may ask why 50? Well, God spoke to me and reminded me about the year of Jubilee, (read the entire chapter of Leviticus 25), and of my own experiences and told me to share these 50 scriptures. However, always believe, know, and keep in your heart and mind that God's Word say that ALL scriptures, are given for Inspiration. In fact, you can read the Bible again and again for a lifetime and never exhaust its understanding, wisdom, and knowledge.

Remember, these are the 50 that God gave me to share with you. When you complete these 50, and believe you are in permanent possession of them, I ask that you continue to read, study and explore these scriptures further as there are many others that will feed your spirit with the same positive effects. Some of these are also specific scriptures God gave me to stand on daily in my walk with Him.

Some suggestions for using this Spiritual Guide are:

1). Read it through at one reading to get the overall impact of some of the 50 awesome gems ever spoken.

2). Memorize one verse a day. Meditate on the message I gave with each scripture.

3). It is possible that some may have a greater stronger effect on you than others depending on your situation. If this is the case, I suggest you highlight it. Keep this spiritual guide, with you at all times, especially at work, so you can read it until the Words of God dominate your thoughts.

4). Read them before you go to bed and when you awake.

I do not have the scriptures arranged according to importance, nor your problem(s). All of God's scriptures are important, because they are all given for inspiration. I am writing them in the order God gave them to me. I deliver them to you with my prayer and hope that these 50 Revitalizing Inspirational Thought Conditioners may add to your JOY and change your way of thinking everyday in the Name of Jesus.

Amen

1

Trust in the Lord with all thine heart; and lean not unto thine own understanding. In all thy ways acknowledge Him, and He shall direct thy paths.

Proverbs 3:5-6

This is one of the scriptures that God has me to stand on daily. This scripture will keep you from stressing out and worrying about what is going to happen on tomorrow or the next day or any day. When we have an important decision to make, we sometime feel that we can't trust anyone...not even God at times. But God knows what is best for us. He is a better judge of what we need than we are!

We must trust Him completely in every choice we make. Bring our decisions to

God in prayer, use the Bible as your guide; and then follow God's leading.

2

*For God hath not given us the spirit
of fear; but of power, and of love
and a sound mind.*

II Timothy 1:7

This is one of the scriptures that God gave me to stand on when feeling fearful or anxious. Your fears can be healed through reading and believing this scripture daily. It tells us that fear is overcome by power. You may ask what is power? There is only one force that is more powerful than fear and that is faith in God. When fear comes to your mind, counteract it by saying what God said through faith. Then the next step to know is that love overcomes fear. Love means to trust, have confidence and complete dependence upon God. Remember, God shed His precious blood for all of our sins. Practice this principle and fear will disappear from you.

3

God is our refuge and strength, a very present help in trouble.

Psalms 46:1

When trouble seems to be on every side, and you need comfort and protection as well as the strength to be able to stand up to it and meet the challenge before us. The Bible is clear regarding this. God is our refuge even in the face of total destruction. He is not merely a temporary retreat: He is our eternal refuge, and can provide strength in any circumstances.

4

*Come unto me, all ye labor
and are heavy laden, and I will
give you rest*

Matthew 11:28

Just maybe that you are feeling tired from the burden and strain of life, and you feel weighed down. Your load seems so heavy that you feel you cannot bear it. If so; perhaps, you are more focus on your problem(s) than your promise. Let me challenge you to "lighten up" in life. Don't take things so seriously. Lighten up and laugh more. Allow this scripture to marinate deep in your thoughts and spirit.

Primarily, we do not get tired in our muscles, but in our minds. So whatever controls the mind controls the person. As you guard your thoughts and focus on Jesus more, He will give you rest. God says, "Learn of Me" A relationship with God changes meaningless toil into spiritual productivity and purpose. That is to say, you can RELAX in Jesus.

5

And He said; The things which are impossible with men are possible with God.

Luke 18:27

Right here, God will show us how to do the "impossible" if we allow Him to do it. Get a grip on your problem and declare the Word of God. Because money represents power, authority, and success, often it is difficult for wealthy people to realize their need and their powerlessness to save themselves The rich, who is talented or intelligent, suffers the same difficulty. Unless God reaches down into their lives, they will not come to Him. It is difficult for a self-sufficient person to realize sometimes the need to come to Jesus, but "the things which are impossible with men are possible with God."

6

And Jesus answering saith unto them, Have faith in God.

Mark 11:22

The kind of prayer that moves mountains is prayer for the fruitfulness of God's Kingdom. God will answer your prayers, but not as a result of your positive mental attitude alone. Other conditions must be met.

- You must be a believer.
- You must not hold a grudge against another person.
- You must not pray with selfish motives.
- Your request must be for the good of the Kingdom. For example, if you are praying to become a multi-millionaire, you need to check your real motive behind why you are asking.

28

7

A soft answer turneth away wrath,
but grievous words stir up anger.

Proverbs 15:1

Have you ever tried to argue in a whisper? It is equally hard to argue with someone who insists on answering softly.

On the other hand, a rising voice and harsh words almost always trigger an angry response. To turn away wrath and seek peace, quiet words are your best choice. By doing what God said here, does not make us weak, but wise in our doing.

This can ONLY be done through Jesus Christ.

8

O taste and see that the Lord is good: blessed is the man that trusteth in Him.

Psalms 34:8

"Taste and see" does not mean, "Check out God's credentials." Instead it is a warm invitation: "Try this, I know you'll like it." When we take that first step of obedience in following God, we cannot help discovering that He is good and kind. When we begin the Christian life, our knowledge of God is partial and incomplete. But as we begin to trust Him daily, we experience how good He is.

9

The Lord is my light and my salvation; whom shall I fear? the Lord is the strength of my life; of whom shall I be afraid?

Psalms 27:1

Fear is a dark shadow that envelopes us and ultimately imprisons us within ourselves. Probably all of us have experience fear at one time or another: fear of rejection, fear of being misunderstood, fear of uncertainty, fear of sickness, or even death. But we can conquer fear by using the bright liberating light of the Lord who brings salvation. If we want to dispel the darkness of fear, we need to remember what the psalmist said, "The Lord is my light and my salvation." He will always be there for you.

31

10

*The Lord is my Shepherd; I
shall not want*

Psalms 23:1

As the Lord is the good shepherd, so we are His sheep...not dumb, frightened, passive animals, but obedient followers, who are wise enough to follow one who will lead us in right places and in right ways. This psalm does not focus on the animal-like qualities of sheep, but on the discipleship qualities of those who follow. When we allow God, our shepherd, to guide us, we have contentment. When we choose to sin, however, we go our own way and cannot blame God for the environment we create for ourselves. When you recognize the good shepherd, follow Him!!

11

He that dwelleth in the secret place
of the most High shall abide under
the shadow of the Almighty.

Psalm 91:1

God is a refuge, a shelter when we are afraid. Our faith in God as a protector will carry us through all dangers and fears in life. This should be a picture of our trust...trading all our fears for faith in Him, no matter the intensity of them. However, to do this, we must "dwell" or "abide" with Him relinquishing ourselves to His protection and pledging our daily devotion to Him -- we will be kept safe.

12

*Than Job arose, and rent his mantle,
and shaved his head and fell down upon
the ground, and worshipped, And said,
Naked came I out of my mother's womb,
and Naked shall I return thither: the
Lord gave, and the Lord hath taken
away; blessed be the name of the Lord.*

Job 1:20-21

Have you ever lost something or someone that you really loved -- maybe a diamond or a closed family member like a child, mother or father? Well, Job did!! He lost his possessions and family in this first of Satan's tests against him. Job did not hide his overwhelming grief. Nor did he lose his faith in God. Instead, his emotions showed that he was human and that he loved his family. God created our emotions, and it is not sinful or inappropriate to express them as Job did. If you have experienced a deep loss, a disappointment, or a heart break, admit your feelings to yourself and others and grieve. Job reacted rightly toward God in his grief by acknowledging God's sovereign authority over everything God had given him. Job passed the test and proved that people can love God for who He is, not for what He gives. We, too, can pass this test just as Job did, but we need to know and understand that God is really in control of everything and submit our will to His.

13

Peace I leave with you, my peace I give unto you: not as the world giveth, give I unto you. Let not your heart be troubled neither let it be afraid.

John 14:27

In the midst of all that is going on in the world, we still should have a deep quietness inside of our belly. But you can only get this peace through God that is available to every believer. Without this peace we become worried and tensed, which can lead to health problems as well. To avoid this, we should think only on the good and perfect things of God. Focus your mind onto some of God's beauty that only He could make and perfect (i. e. beautiful sunset, waterfall flowing down, or a beautiful song in your heart).

14

*Create in me a clean heart, O God;
and renew a right spirit within me.*

Psalms 51:10

Because we are born as sinners, our natural inclination is to please ourselves rather than God. David followed that inclination when he took another man's wife in the book of Kings. We also follow it when we sin in any way. Like David, we must ask God to cleanse us from within, clearing our heart and spirit for new thoughts and desires. Right conduct can only come from a clean heart and spirit. Ask God to create in you a clean heart and spirit today. Do not allow another day to pass after you read this that you do not ask God to "Renew a right spirit within me."

15

That if thou shall confess with thy mouth the Lord Jesus, and shalt believe in thine heart that God hath raised Him from the dead, thou shall be saved.

Romans 10:9

Have you ever been asked: How do I become a Christian? What do I need to do? Well, there are many who will make you think you "gotta" jump off tall building and swim the high seas to get saved, but the devil is a liar. God only requires you to confess with your mouth and believe the verse above, then you are saved. Again, people will make you think it is a complicated process, but it is not. If we believe in our hearts and say with our mouths that Christ is the risen Lord, we will be saved. Now give God some praise.

16

The thief cometh not, but for to steal, and to kill, and to destroy: I am come that they might have life, and that they might have it more abundantly.

John 10:10

There are many people in the world that lack energy because they are not sure where it comes from. For many, they compare themselves to the energizer bunny on the TV commercial that runs on a Duracell battery that says it keeps going...and going...and going, and all of a sudden you hear it getting weak and running out of energy. In contrast, to the thief who takes, Jesus gives. The life He gives is more abundantly richer and fuller. It is eternal; yet, it begins immediately. Life in Him is lived on a higher plain because of his overflowing forgiveness, love, and guidance. The way to an energized life is Christ Jesus. Make this one of your daily confession. Christ has come that I (say your name) might have life and might have it more abundantly.

17

*What shall we say to these things? If
God be for us; who can be against us?*

Romans 8:31

Just imagine yourself looking at all your
problems like an army lined up against
you. Then I want you to realize that you
have a Father in heaven that can
overcome them all. So, as you face your
enemies...sickness,   discouragement,
finances, disappointment, frustrations,
weaknesses, hostility, ask yourself the
question God ask, 'What shall I say to
these things?," and then give the answer
God gave us, "If God be for us, who can
be against us?" He will not withhold any
good thing from us.

18

Confess your faults one to another, and pray one for another, that ye may be healed. The effectual fervent prayer of a righteous man availeth much.

James 5:16

If you have sickness in your body, God is a healer. God heals through your faith in Him. Little faith equals little power, much faith equals much power. Confession is very important in all we do, especially healing because much illness is a result of buried resentments, unforgiveness, and guilt. Being effectual fervent is a very powerful prayer of faith. Christ has made it possible for us to go directly to God for forgiveness.

19

*Now faith is the substance of things
hoped for; the evidence of
things not seen.*

Hebrews 11:1

This is one of the scriptures that God gave me to stand on. Do you remember how you felt when your birthday was approaching? You were excited and anxious. You just knew that you were going to receive gifts and other special treats -- birthdays combined assurance anticipation, and so does faith! You have to say before you see. God spoke the worlds into existence through words before seeing it. This is what we need to do. We have to have faith and believe what we have asked God for in the spirit shall manifest in the natural before you even see it. Now, give God some praise for that new car you need and have faith and believe what you said and watch it come to pass.

20

*But He was wounded for our
transgressions, He was bruised for
our iniquities: the chastisement of
our peace was upon Him: and with
His stripes we are healed.*

Isaiah 53:5

How could an Old Testament person understand the idea of Christ dying for our sin--actually bearing the punishment that we deserved But God was pulling aside the curtain of time to let the people of Isaiah's day look ahead to the suffering of the future Messiah and the resulting forgiveness made available to all mankind. I know He is a healer, because I am a living witness. If He did it for me, He will do it for you. God is not a respecter of persons.

21

*Now unto to Him that is able to do
exceeding abundantly above all that
we ask or think, according to the
power that worketh in us.*

Ephesians 3:20

You know how we see or get something, and we look at it and say, "This is too good to be true." But we must realize that with God nothing is too good to be true. We must have the understanding that our most wonderful dreams can come true. All that we need, we can have. If we are living outside of God's will, resolve to stop it today, and start expecting great things to happen to you. God wants to bless us abundantly, so let's not hinder His generosity.

46

22

Ask, and it shall be given you; seek, and ye shall find; knock, and it shall be opened unto you.

Matthew 7:7

Jesus tells us in the Word of God to persist and pursue God. People often give up after a few halfhearted efforts and conclude that God cannot be found. But knowing God takes faith, focus, and follow through. Jesus assures us that our efforts will be rewarded when we seek God. One reason we do not get answers to our prayers is that we ask, but do not expect to receive. The spiritual protocol that God has given us is to ask, and then immediately believe we are already receiving it.

23

Brethren, I count not myself to have apprehended: but this one thing I do, forgetting those things which are behind, and reaching forth unto those things which are before, I press toward the mark for the prize of the high calling in Christ Jesus.

Philippians 3:13-14

Every one of us, if we are to live successfully, we must leave past failures and mistakes behind and move forward without allowing them to become a weight in our lives. And every night before you lie down, practice leaving the past in the past, and look unto Jesus, the author and finisher of our faith.

24

*Be careful for nothing; but in every
thing by prayer and supplication
with thanksgiving let your requests
be made known unto God.*

Philippians 4:6

"Be careful for nothing" means don't worry. Imagine never worrying about anything! Wow, I know this might seems like an impossibility, but we need to practice turning our worries into prayers. Do you want to worry less? Then pray more! Whenever you start to worry, stop and pray.

25

*Children, obey your parents in the
Lord: for this is right.*

Ephesians 6:1

There is a difference between obeying and honoring. To obey means to do as one is told; to honor means to respect and love. Children are not commanded to disobey God as obeying their parents. Adult children are not asked to be subservient to domineering parents. Children are to obey while under their parents care, but the responsibility to honor parents is for life.

26

Finally, my brethren, be strong in the Lord, and in the power of His might.

Ephesians 6:10

In the Christian life we battle against "Principalities and powers" (the evil powerful forces of fallen angels headed by Satan who is a vicious fighter). To withstand their attacks, we must depend on God's strength and use every piece of His armor. Our whole body needs to be armed. As we do battle against the rulers of darkness of this world, fight in the strength of the Christ, whose power comes from the Holy Spirit.

27

---

*But this I say, he which soweth
sparingly shall reap also sparingly:
and he which soweth bountifully
shall reap also bountifully.*

2 Corinthians 9:6

Many people hesitate to give generously to God if they worry about having enough money left over to meet their own needs. We are assured by God that He will meet every one of our needs. But the person who gives only a little will receive only a little in return. Don't let your lack of faith keep you from giving freely and generously.

28

*Neither shall they say, Lo here! or
lo there! for, behold, the kingdom of
God is within you.*

Luke 17:21

The Pharisees asked Jesus when God's Kingdom would come, not knowing that it had already arrived. The Kingdom of God is not like an earthly kingdom with geographical boundaries. Instead, it begins with the work of God's Spirit in people's lives and relationships. Still today, we must resist looking to institutions or programs for evidence of the progress of God's Kingdom. Instead, we should look for what God is doing in people's heart. When you are filled with self- doubt, and don't know which way to turn, remember, we have the Kingdom of God inside of us if we are a believer. Therefore, we have POWER inside of us. We only have to believe in ourselves, and the strength within us will be released.

29

There is therefore now no condemnation to them which are in Christ Jesus, who walk not after the flesh, but after the Spirit.

Romans 8:1

"Not guilty, let him go free"...what would those words mean to us if we were on death row? The fact is that the whole human race is on death row, justly condemned for repeatedly breaking God's holy Law. But without Jesus we would have no hope at all. Thanks be to God that He has declared us not guilty and has offered us freedom from sin and "POWER" to do His will.

A friend and I was talking about Jesus one day as we always do, and she brought out an excellent point regarding this very subject during our conversation. I like the way she stated it.

She exclaimed to me that Grace and Mercy are TWINS. Then she went on to explain this further. "Grace" is when God gives us what we don't deserve; Mercy is when God doesn't give us what we do deserve. I thought that was very well said.

30

*Steps of a good man are ordered by
the Lord.*

Psalm 37:23

A believer is one who follows God, trusts Him, and tries to do His will. When we do, God watches over us and directs every step we take. If you would like to have God direct your way, then seek His advice before you step out.

31

Fret not thyself because of evildoers, neither be thou envious against the workers on iniquity.

Psalm 37:1

We should never envy the wicked, even though some may be extremely popular or excessively rich. No matter how much they have, it will fade and vanish like a vapor of hot air and disappear. Those who follow God live differently from the wicked, and in the end have far greater treasurers in heaven. What unbelievers may achieve may last a long time, if they have been good stewards, but what we get from following God lasts forever. SELAH!!

32

*I will bless the Lord at all times; His
praise shall continually
be in my mouth.*

Psalm 34:1

When we praise God, it brings us into His presence and we can feel how close we are to Him. I'm reminded of the song "Praise is what I do when I wanna get close to you." If you need anything from God, just give Him a shout out. You can even cry out to Him and say Jesus...Jesus...Jesus...either way, He will come see about you. If you need something from God, remember your breakthrough is in your praise. Practice this daily and watch how God comes to rescue you.

33

Declare His glory among the heathen, His wonders among all people.

Psalm 96:3

If we believe God is great, we cannot help telling others about Him. The best witnessing happens when our hearts are full of appreciation for what He has done. God has chosen to use us to declare His wonders among all people. God "overflows" from His creation and should overflow from our lips. Question? How well are you doing at telling others about God's goodness and greatness? It's still not too late.

34

Pray without Ceasing

I Thessalonians 5:17

It is impossible to spend all of our time on our knees, but it is possible to have a prayerful attitude at all times. This attitude is built upon acknowledging our dependence on God, realizing His presence within us, and determining to obey Him fully. Then we will find it is natural to pray frequent, spontaneous, short prayers. A prayerful attitude is not a substitute for regular times of prayer, but should be an outgrowth of those times.

35

Beloved, believe not every spirit, but try the spirits whether they are of God: because many false prophets are gone out into the world.

I John 4:1

"Believe not every spirit, but try the spirits" means we should not believe everything we hear just because someone says it is a message inspired by God. There are many ways to test people to see if their message is truly from God.

One is to check their words with what God says in the Bible. Other tests include their commitment to the body of believers (1 John 2:19), their lifestyle (1 John 3:23-24), and the fruit of their ministry (1 John 4:6).

But the most important test of all, says John, is what they believe about Christ. Do they teach that Jesus is fully God and Fully man? Our world is filled with voices claiming to speak to God. Make sure you give them these tests to see if they are indeed speaking God's truth.

36

Beloved, I wish above all thing that thou mayest prosper and be in health, even as thy soul prospereth.

III John 1:2

God gave us as believers a three-fold covenant in the above scripture. (1) He wants us to prosper in every area of our life. (2) He wants us to be in good health with no sickness in our body, and (3) He wants our soul to prosper. We should be concerned about both our body and soul. As responsible Christians, we should neither neglect or indulge ourselves, but care for our physical needs as well as discipline our bodies so we are at our best for God's service.

37

For God so loved the world, that He gave His only begotton son, that whosoever believeth in Him should not perish, but have everlasting life.

John 3:16

God sent His only son to Calvary to die in our place for our sins because He loved us so much. This should be enough alone to make us strive with both intrinsic and extrinsic drive to do His will, so we will live with Him forever. In eternal life there is no death, sickness, enemy, evil, or sin. When we don't know Christ, we make choices as though this life were all we had. In reality, this life is just the introduction to eternity. Meditate on this scripture daily and imagine Jesus on the cross dying for our sins and then receive this new life by faith and begin to evaluate all that happens from an eternal perspective.

38

Thou shall guide me with thy counsel, and afterward receive me to glory.

Psalm 73:24

God has answers to all our problems. Therefore, put all your problems in God's hands and He will give you the right answer (s). From birth to death, God has us continually in His grip. But far more, we have the hope of the resurrection.

Though our courage and strength may fail, we know that one day we will be raised to life to serve Him forever. He is our security and we must cling to Him.

39

Not that I speak in respect of want:
for I have learned, in whatsoever
state I am in therewith to be content.

Philippians 4:11

Even though you may not like your present situation, put the matter in God's hands and if He wants you someplace else, He will lead you there. But it could be that He wants you where you are. In that case He will help you to adjust to the situation. He will make you content, or even grateful for the present opportunities. Learn this principle of doing the best you can, with what you have, where you are.

When you do this, you learn how to make your present situation a better one.

40

Rejoice Evermore

I Thessalonians 5:16

Our joy, prayers, and thankfulness to God should not fluctuate with our circumstances or feelings. Obeying these three commands: rejoice, keep praying, and give thanks, often, goes against our natural inclinations, but we must do it, if we want to walk in victory everyday in our lives. When we make a conscious decision to do what the Word says, we will begin to see people and things in a new perspective. When we do God's will, we will find it easier to be joyful and thankful.

41

But of that day and that hour no man knoweth, no man, no, not the angels which are in heaven, neither the son, but the Father.

Mark 13:32

Almost yearly, there arises someone declaring they know when the end is going to come. In 2010, there were billboard signs throughout the nation that someone put up declaring this. This kind of misleading foolishness has become very prominent in the media nowadays. But real Christians already know, this is folly--a ploy of Satan to deter us from our walk with God. And to get us to believe something that God already made very plain and clear to us in the scripture.

The emphasis on this verse is not on Jesus' lack of knowledge, but rather on the fact that no one knows. It is God, the Father's, secret to be revealed when He desires. No one can predict by scripture or science the exact day of Jesus' return. Jesus is teaching that preparation, not calculation, is needed. I caution every born again believer to believe the Word of God and not man.

42

*He must increase, but
I must decrease.*

John 3:30

When we as believers are willing to decrease in importance then this shows unusual humility. Many Pastors and other Christian leaders can be tempted to focus more on the success of their ministries than on Christ. Beware of those who put more emphasis on their own achievements than on God's Kingdom.

43

*Moreover it is required in stewards,
that a man be found faithful.*

1 Corinthians 4:2

A servant does what his master tells him to do. If we as servants, though faith, believe that Jesus is our Master, then we should want to do what He tells us to do. As servants, we must do what God tells us to do in the Bible and through His Holy Spirit. Each day God presents us with needs and opportunities that challenge us to do what we know is right.

44

Bring ye all the tithes into the storehouse, that there may be meat in mine house, and prove me now herewith, saith the Lord of hosts, if I will not open you the windows of heaven, and pour you out a blessing, that there shall not be room enough to receive it.

Malachi 3:10

Are you a tither? Or are you one of those persons who use to tithe and decided since you now have made so many bills, you will stop tithing and start again later. Well, let me help you out before you self-destruct, like I did many years ago. It does not work. God even asked the question, "Will a man rob God?" Well as I said, I did it, but I was ignorant of the Word. Many were saying to me that I do not need to do that as God will still bless me. I could see that He definitely was, as I was still living and breathing, but they left some very important information off. I say they withheld the best information from me. But, I'm not mad at them, because it is possible that they did not understand this Kingdom principle either.

Well, I started reading and getting into the Word of God more and more for myself, and this is when God revealed the powerful truth above to me. After that I could not wait to get paid and get to the church to pay my tithes. If you are not doing this, it's not too late. Start today and through faith watch God open up the windows of heaven for you and pour you out a blessing that you will not have room enough to receive. Trust God everyday no matter what it looks like.

45

Bless them that curse you, and pray for them which despitefully use you.

Luke 6:28

A forgiving spirit demonstrates that a person has received God's forgiveness. If we are critical rather than compassionate, we will also receive criticism. If we treat others generously, graciously, and compassionately, however, these qualities will come back to us in full measure. I am a living witness. We are to love others, not judge them.

46

*For we all have sinned, and come
short of the glory of God.*

Romans 3:23

Some sins seem bigger than others because their obvious consequences are much more serious and visible. Murder, for example, seems to us to be worst than hatred, and adultery seems worst than lust. But this does not mean that because we do sins that are less serious or less visible, we deserve eternal life. All sin makes us sinners, and all sin cuts us off from our Holy God. All sin, therefore, leads to death (because it disqualifies us from living with God, regardless of how great or small it seems). Don't minimize "little" sins or overrate "big" sins. They all separate us from God, but they all can be forgiven.

47

And above all things have fervent charity among yourselves: for charity shall cover the multitude of sins.

I Peter 4:8

God wants us to continually grow in love for one another. If we claim to know something about someone we do not love, what do we do with this information? Do we go and tell others, so they can gossip about it as well and start some "mess?" Or do we handle it as God has command us to do. Remember we have all done something, so it is important to pray regularly. Our possessions, status, and power will mean nothing in God's Kingdom, but you will spend eternity with other people. Let us invest our time and talents where they will make an eternal difference.

48

(For we walk by faith, not by sight):

II Corinthians 5:7

As I reflect back over my own life, I cannot only see what God has done for me in the natural, but in hindsight, I can see what God has done for me in the past. I also now see in the spirit realm what He is and will do for me in the future. This can only come through faith in God. We, as Christian believers, cannot afford to walk by what we see before us. If we do, we will be depressed everyday living in this world.

We see the rising gas and food prices, but if we walk by faith, we would just pull up to the pump, fill our vehicles up, and pay the attendance. Why? Because we understand what faith in God really is. I challenge all of you to read and meditate on this scripture until it is embedded deep in your spirit and then walk confidently in it.

49

*We are confident, I say, and willing
rather to be absent from the body,
and to be present with the Lord.*

II Corinthians 5:8

Paul said for him to live is Christ, and to die is gain. He was not afraid to die because he was confident of spending eternity with Christ. Although, facing the unknown may cause us anxiety and leave loved ones hurts deeply, but if we believe in Jesus Christ, we can share Paul's hope and confidence of eternal life with Christ in the great resurrection.

50

*It is a good thing to give thanks unto
the Lord, and to sing praises unto
thy name O most High.*

Psalm 92:1

Especially during the Thanksgivings holiday, we focus on our blessings and expressing our gratitude to God for them. But thanks should be on our lips daily. We can never say thank you enough to parents, friends, leaders, and especially to God. When thanksgiving becomes an integral part of our life, we will find that our attitude toward life will change. We will become more positive, gracious, and humble.

To order more copies of this book,
please visit our website:

www.janwhitaker.info

www.ingramcontent.com/pod-product-compliance
Lightning Source LLC
Chambersburg PA
CBHW051849040426
42447CB00006B/767